Size

Julie Murray

Abdo Kids Junior
is an Imprint of Abdo Kids
abdobooks.com

Abdo
MEASURE IT!
Kids

abdobooks.com

Published by Abdo Kids, a division of ABDO, P.O. Box 398166, Minneapolis, Minnesota 55439.
Copyright © 2020 by Abdo Consulting Group, Inc. International copyrights reserved in all countries.
No part of this book may be reproduced in any form without written permission from the publisher.
Abdo Kids Junior™ is a trademark and logo of Abdo Kids.

Printed in the United States of America, North Mankato, Minnesota.

052019

092019

THIS BOOK CONTAINS
RECYCLED MATERIALS

Photo Credits: iStock, Shutterstock

Production Contributors: Teddy Borth, Jennie Forsberg, Grace Hansen

Design Contributors: Christina Doffing, Candice Keimig, Dorothy Toth

Library of Congress Control Number: 2018963323

Publisher's Cataloging-in-Publication Data

Names: Murray, Julie, author.

Title: Size / by Julie Murray.

Description: Minneapolis, Minnesota : Abdo Kids, 2020 | Series: Measure it! |
    Includes online resources and index.

Identifiers: ISBN 9781532185304 (lib. bdg.) | ISBN 9781532186288 (ebook) |
    ISBN 9781532186776 (Read-to-me ebook)

Subjects: LCSH: Size and shape--Juvenile literature. | Size perception--Juvenile
    literature. | Measurement--Juvenile literature.

Classification: DDC 530.813--dc23

Table of Contents

Size

Size tells us how big or small something is.

To find size, we can **compare** things.

The dog is big. The kitten is little.

BIG

little

9

Sam is short. Her dad is tall.

tall

short

11

The book is **thick**.

The paper is thin.

thick / thin

13

Lily has long hair.

Jack has short hair.

short
I

long

15

The elephant is **huge**.

Her calf is small.

HUGE

small

The zebra is tall. The elephant is taller. The giraffe is the tallest.

taller

tallest

tall

Which one is bigger? The clown
fish or the yellow fish?

Let's Review!

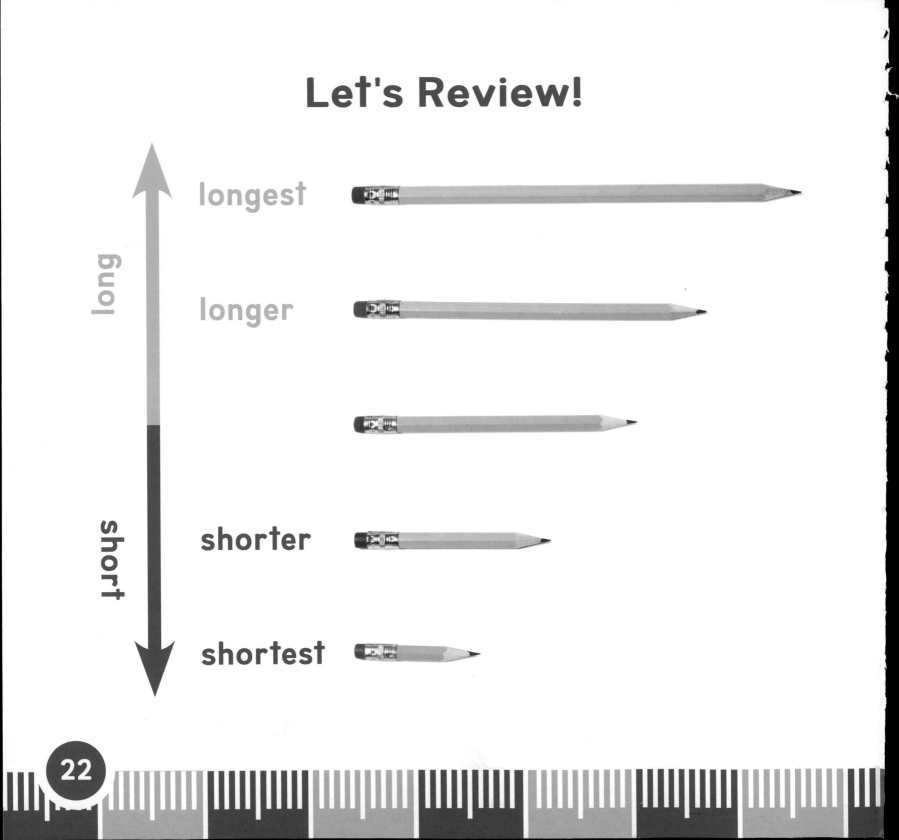

Glossary

huge
of very large weight or size.

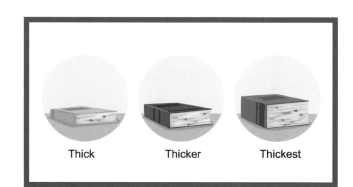

compare
to note the similarities or
differences of.

thick
large in measurement from one
side to the other.

Index

Abdo Kids
ONLINE
FREE! ONLINE MULTIMEDIA RESOURCES

Visit **abdokids.com**
to access crafts, games,
videos, and more!

Use Abdo Kids code

MSK5304

or scan this QR code!